T0013565

With thanks to Willy and Oliver Willems

For . . . buzz, buzz . . . Olivia and Lialotta

FSC
www.fsc.org
MIX
Paper from
responsible sources
FSC® C118365

Copyright © 2022 Clavis Publishing Inc., New York

Originally published as *De imker* in Belgium and the Netherlands by Clavis Uitgeverij, 2016
English translation from the Dutch by Clavis Publishing Inc., New York

Visit us on the Web at www.clavis-publishing.com.

No part of this publication may be reproduced or stored in a retrieval system,
or transmitted in any form or by any means, electronic, mechanical, photocopying,
recording, or otherwise, without the prior written permission of the publisher,
except in the case of brief quotations embodied in critical articles and reviews.
For information regarding permissions, write to Clavis Publishing, info-US@clavisbooks.com.

Beekeepers and What They Do written and illustrated by Liesbet Slegers

ISBN 978-1-60537-803-9

This book was printed in August 2022 at Nikara,
M. R. Štefánika 858/25, 963 01 Krupina, Slovakia.

First Edition
10 9 8 7 6 5 4 3 2 1

Clavis Publishing supports the First Amendment and celebrates the right to read.

Beekeepers

and What They Do

Liesbet Slegers

Clavis

NEW YORK

Apples grow on trees, and strawberries grow on plants.
Bees help make that happen. They fly around in search
of pollen and nectar to eat. When they buzz from flower
to flower, the pollen sticks to their bodies and fertilizes
other little flowers and fruits and vegetables so they grow.
So, we really need bees!

The pollen sticks to her body.

The bee sucks nectar.

Bees are friendly animals. They only sting when protecting
their nest. The beekeeper helps take care of them.
She wears a special suit that protects her from bee stings.
Because bees are attracted to colors, her suit is white.
It has a hood with netting that lets her see and breathe.
She also wears long gloves and plastic boots to cover her hands
and feet. This way, she's completely protected from head to toe!

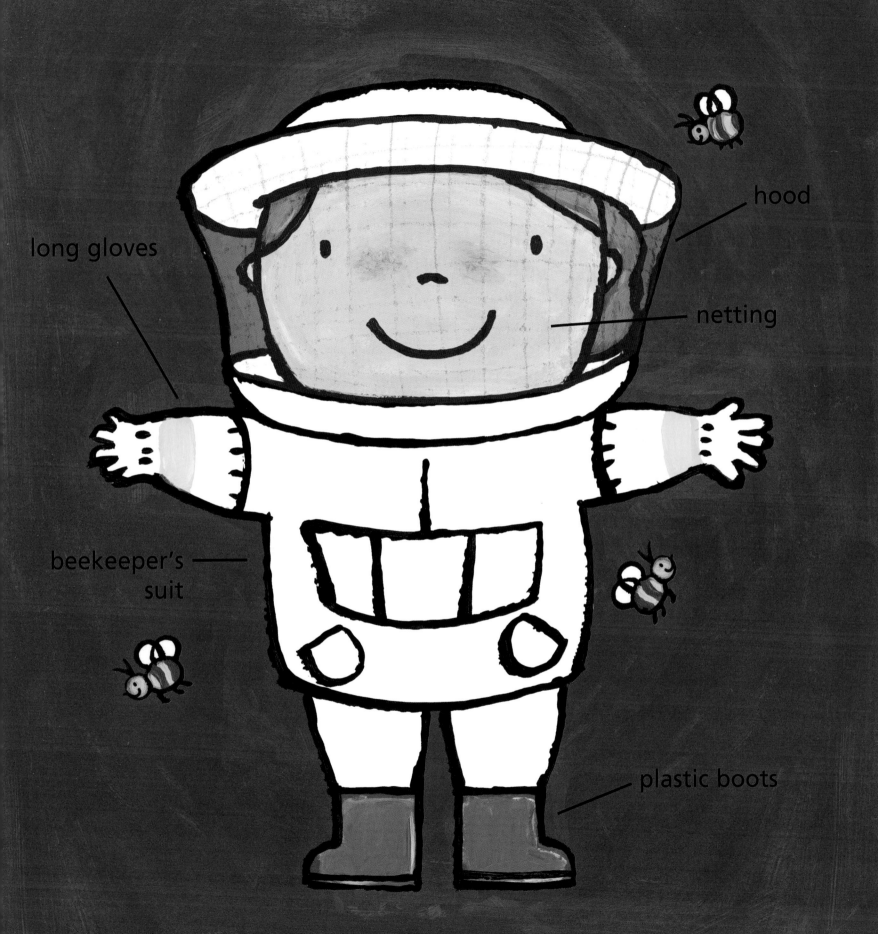

long gloves

hood

netting

beekeeper's
suit

plastic boots

The smoke that comes out of the smoker calms the bees.

The bees live in a beehive, where they turn nectar into honey and store it in honeycombs. Honeycombs are like little jars of wax. When there's lots of honey, the beekeeper opens the hive and removes the frames, which hold the honeycombs. To calm the bees, she distributes smoke and then gently brushes off the little insects with a feather or a soft brush. Then she takes the frames to the extractor to harvest the honey. Yummy!

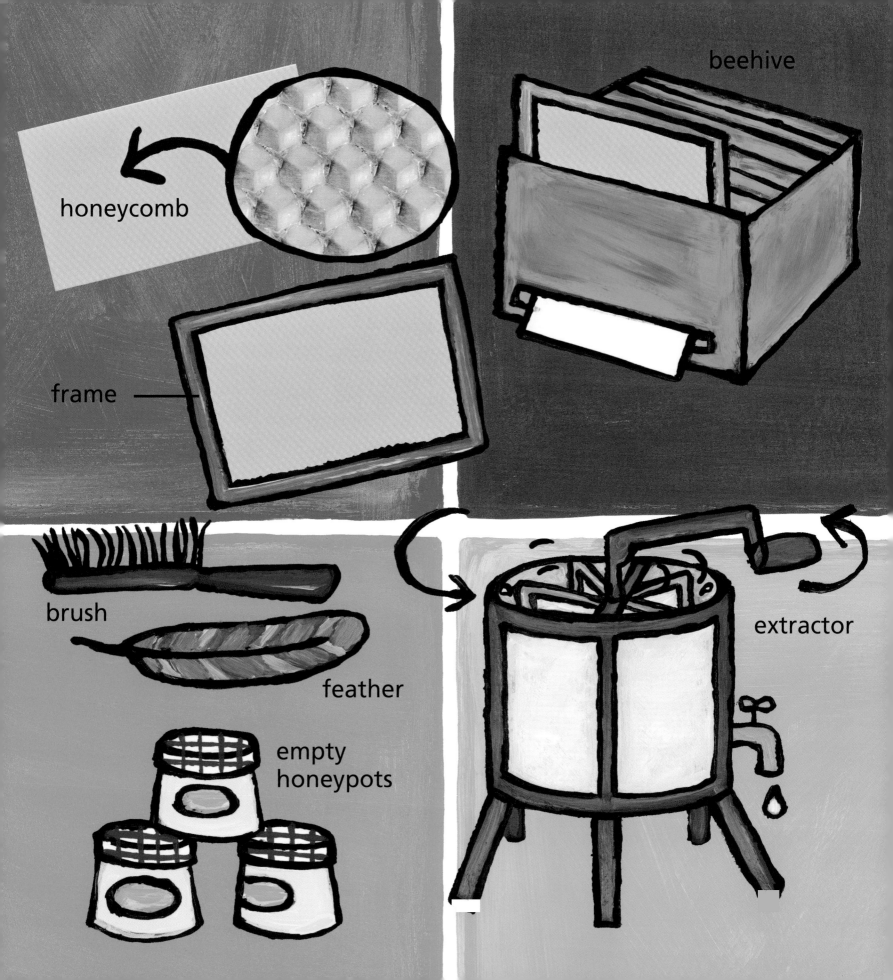

honeycomb

beehive

frame

brush

feather

empty honeypots

extractor

With the brush, the beekeeper carefully sweeps the bees from the frames.

It's spring and the sun is shining. The flowers are blooming,
and the buds are opening on the trees. They smell delicious.
This makes the bees happy and wakes them up! Buzz, buzz!
After a long, cold winter, the frames need a spring cleaning.
The beekeeper removes the old, empty frames and puts in
clean new ones. Now the bees can start making honey again.

Bees are flying out of the beehive looking for
flowers and nectar. When the bees return to the hive,
they turn the nectar into honey. They store the pollen and
honey in the combs so they have something to eat later on.
The bees have one queen. She's bigger than the other bees and
always stays in the hive. She lays eggs in the small bowls of the comb.
After a while the larvae become bees. Buzz, buzz! What a bustle!

comb

honey

filling with honey

a grain of pollen

pollen

queen

laying eggs

feeding the larvae

When the beekeeper wants to have a look inside the hive, she gently blows smoke into it. The bees become calm and aren't afraid. That's why they don't sting her. The beekeeper checks on the young bees. Are they healthy and growing well? She lets the peaceful bees stay on the frame. It's fun to see lots of bees together!

The hive is getting crowded, so some of the bees go in search of a new home. First the hive needs a new queen to stay back with some of the bees. The old queen leaves with all the other bees. They follow her wherever she goes! Before the bees leave, they eat until their bellies are full. That's clever, because they don't know how quickly they'll find a new home. Look! There they go! Buzz, buzz! Have a safe journey!

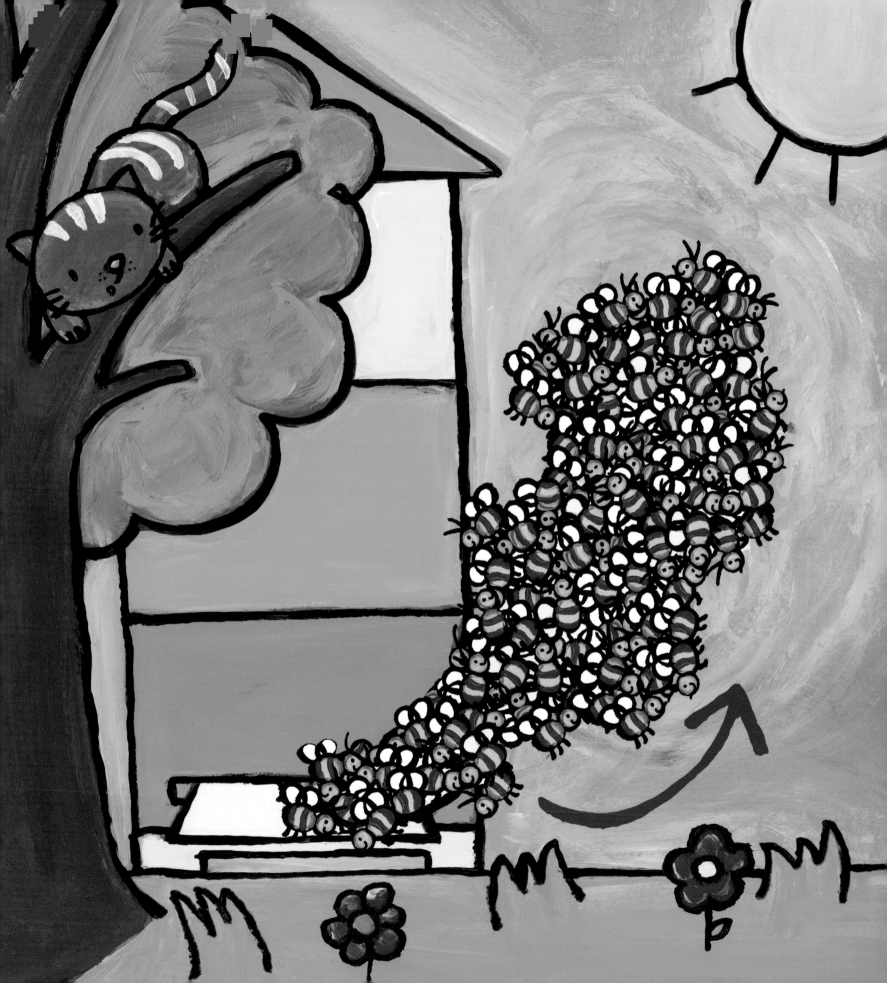

The beekeeper keeps a careful eye on the bees. Any moment, a bunch of bees can fly out. Look! A swarm of them has landed on a branch in a cherry tree. The beekeeper puts them in a special basket called a skep. Now she can take them home. Gee, a swarm has clustered on a bicycle wheel. Luckily, the bees ate well and are calm. The beekeeper will come along with a skep to take them home. Thanks, beekeeper!

skep

The honey super is a storage box at the top of the hive.

The bees are working hard! The frames in the honey super are full of honey. The beekeeper takes out the frames and carefully sweeps off the bees that are on it. When there's a little smoke, they don't mind. The beekeeper leaves the frames in the lower storage. That's where the bees live, and they need the sweets when it gets cold and there are no flowers anymore.

empty
honey super

The beekeeper puts the frames in the extractor. When she cranks the handle, the honey-covered frames spin around, and the sweet liquid is flung out and collects at the bottom of the tank. Soon, it's filled with honey! Now it has to settle a little. Every now and then, the beekeeper stirs it. After a while, she can open the small tap and fill the honeypots. It's ready to enjoy!

Autumn has come, and it's getting chilly out. The bees want
to collect as much food as possible before winter sets in.
Meanwhile, the beekeeper cleans the honey super frames
by removing the old pollen and wax. Now everything is
ready for next spring! The beekeeper can make candles
out of the leftover beeswax. That's nice!

Now winter has come, and it's very cold outside. The beekeeper stays in her cozy home. Honey is delicious on a piece of toast or in a cup of tea. It's also very healthy! And what do the bees do in the winter? They stay inside their hives, nice and warm. They feast on the honey they made during the summer.

Bees are important and fascinating small animals.
Would you like to help them?
Grow flowers in your garden.
Then you'll have a lot of humming fun!